A BRIEF ACCOUNT

OF THE

RELIGION & CIVIL INSTITUTIONS

OF THE

BURMANS;

AND

A DESCRIPTION OF THE

KINGDOM OF ASSAM,

FORMERLY PART OF THE EMPIRE OF AVA,

UNDER THE KING OF PEGUE,

TRANSLATED FROM THE ALUMGERNAMEH.

TO WHICH IS ADDED,

AN ACCOUNT OF THE

PETROLEUM WELLS,

IN THE

BURMAH DOMINIONS,

*Extracted from a Journal from Rangoon up the River
Eraiwaddy to Amarapoorah, the present Capital
of the Burmah Empire.*

❖❖❖

CALCUTTA.

AN ACCOUNT

OF THE

RELIGION AND CIVIL INSTITUTIONS

OF THE

BIRMANS,

From Lt. Colonel Symes's Embassy to Ava.

———

AFTER what has been written, there can be little necessity to inform my readers, that the Birmans are Hindûs : not votaries of Brahma, but sectaries of Buddha, which latter is admitted by Hindûs of all descriptions to be the ninth Avatar*, or descent of the Deity in his capacity of preserver. He reformed the doctrines contained in the Vedas, and severely censured the sacrifice of cattle, or depriving any being of life : he

---

* Sir William Jones on the Gods of Greece, Italy, and India.

A

is called the author of happiness: his place of residence was discovered at Gaya, in Bengal, by the illustrious Amara*, renowned amongst men, " who caused an image of the supreme Buddha to be made, and he worshipped it : Reverence be unto thee in the form of Buddha! reverence be unto thee, Lord of the earth! reverence be unto thee, an incarnation of the Deity! and, eternal one, reverence be unto thee, O God, in the form of Mercy!"

Gotma, or Goutum, according to the Hindûs of India, or Gaudma, among the inhabitants of the more eastern parts, is said† to have been a philosopher, and is

---

* See the translation of a Sanscreet inscription, on a stone found in the temple of Buddha, at Gaya, by Mr. Wilkins. Asiat. Res. Vol. I.

† Sir William Jones on the Gods of Greece, Italy and India.

by the Birmans believed to have flourished above 2300* years ago : he taught, in
the Indian schools the heterodox religion
and philosophy of Buddha. The image
that represents Buddha is called Gaudma,
or Goutum, which is now a commonly received appellation of Buddha himself: this
image is the primary object of worship in
all countries situated between Bengal and
China. The sectaries of Buddha contend
with those of Brahma for the honour of antiquity, and are certainly far more numerous. The Cingalese in Ceylon are Buddhaists of the purest source, and the Birmans acknowledge to have originally received their religion from that island†. It
was brought, say the Rhahaans, first from

---

* This agrees with the account of the Siamese compu-
tation given by Kæmpfer.

† The Birmans call Ceylon, Zehoo.

Zehoo (Ceylon) to Arracan, and thence was introduced into Ava, and probably into China ; for the Birmans assert with confidence that the Chinese are Buddhaists.

This is a curious subject of investigation, and the concurrent testimony of circumstances, added to the opinions of the most intelligent writers, seem to leave little doubt of the fact. It cannot, however, be demonstrated beyond the possibily of dispute, till we shall have acquired a more perfect knowledge of Chinese letters, and a readier access to their repositories of learning. Little can at present be added to the lights cast on the subject by the late Sir William Jones, in his discourse delivered to the Asiatic Society on the Chinese. That great man has expressed his conviction in positive terms, that " Buddha was

unquestionably the Foe of China," and
that he was also the God of Japan, and
the Woden of the Goths; an opinion which
corresponds with, and is perhaps grafted
on the information of the learned and la-
borious Kæmpfer*, corroborated after-

* Speaking of the Budz, or Seaka of the Japanese,
Kæmpfer says, " I have strong reason to believe, both
" from the affinity of the name, and the very nature of this
" religion, that its author and founder is the very same
" person whom the Bramans call Buddha, and believe to
" be the essential spirit of Wishna or their deity, who
" made his ninth appearance in the world under this
" name; the Peguers call him Samana Khutama."
Hist. Japan. Book IV. Ch. 6.

Treating of the introduction of Buddha into China,
the same author says " About the year of Christ 518, one
" Darma, a great saint, and twenty-third successor on
" the holy see of Seaka (Buddha,) came over into China
" from Seiteniseku, as the Japanese writers explain it,
" that is, from that part of the world which lies westward
" with regard to Japan, and laid, properly speaking

wards by his own Researches. On whatever grounds the latter inference rests, it
will not tend to weaken the belief of his
first position, when I observe, that the Chinese deputies, on the occasion of our introduction to the Seredaw or high priest of
the Birman empire, prostrated themselves
before him, and afterwards adored an
image of Goudma, with more religious fer-
vour than mere politeness, or acquiescence
in the customs of another nation, would
have excited: the Bonzes also of China,
like the Rhahaans of Ava, wear yellow as
the sacerdotal colour, and in many of their
customs and ceremonies there may be
traced a striking similitude.

Whatever may be the antiquity of the
worship of Buddha, the wide extent of its

―――――――

"the first firm foundation of the Budsdoism in that
"mighty empire". Book IV. ch. 6.

reception cannot be doubted. The most authentic writer * on the eastern peninsula calls the image of Goudma, as worshipped by the Siamese, Somona-codom : being unacquainted with the language of Siam, which from so short a residence as four months it was impossible he could have acquired, he confounds two distinct words, Somona, and Codom, signifying Codom, or Gaudma, in his incarnate state ; the difference between the letters C and G may easily have arisen from the mode of pronunciation in different countries ; even in the Birman manner of uttering the word, the distinction between these letters is not very clear. The Buddha of the Indians and the Birmans, is pronounced by the Siamese, Pooth, or Pood ; by the vulgar, Poo; which without any violence to probability,

* Loubere.

might be converted by the Chinese into Foe*; the Tamulic termination *en*, as Mr. Chambers remarks, creates striking resemblance between Pooden and the Wooden of the Goths ; every person who has conversed with the natives of India, knows that Buddha is the Dies Mercurii, the Wednesday, or Woden's day, of all Hindûs. Chronology, however, which must always be accepted as a surer guide to truth, than inferences drawn from the resemblance of the words, and etymological reasoning, does not, to my mind, sufficiently establish that Buddha and Woden were the same. The period of the ninth incarnation of Vishnu was long antecedent to the existence of the deified hero

---

* M. Gentil asserts that the Chinese admit, by their own accounts, that Foe, their object of worship, was originally brought from India.

of Scandinavia. Sir William Jones determines the period when Buddha appeared on the earth, to be 1014 years before the birth of Christ. Odin, or Woden, flourished at a period not very distant from our Saviour, and was, according to some, a cotemporary of Pompey and of Julius Cæsar. The author of the Northen Antiquities places him 70 years after the Christian era. Even the Birman Gaudma, conformably to their account, must have lived 500 years before Woden. So immense a space can hardly be supposed to have been overlooked: but if the supposition refers, not to the warrior of the north, but to the original deity Odin, the attributes of the latter are as widely opposed to those of Buddha, who was himself only an incarnation of Vishnu, as the dates are incongruous. The deity, whose doctrines

B

were introduced into Scandinavia, was a
god of terror, and his votaries carried de-
solation and the sword throughout whole
regions; but the Ninth Avatar* brought
the peaceful olive, and came into the world
for the sole purpose of preventing sangui-
nary acts. These apparent inconsistencies
will naturally lead us to hesitate in ackow-
ledging Buddha and Woden to be the
same person: their doctrines are opposite,
and their eras are widely remote.

Had that distinguished genius†, whose
learning so lately illumined the East, been
longer spared for the instruction and delight of mankind, he would probably have
elucidated this obscurity, and have remov-

---

* See the account of the Ninth Avatar, by the Rev.
Mr. Maurice, in his History of Hindustan. Vol. II.
Part 3.

† I need hardly observe that I mean Sir William Jones.

ed the dusky veil that still hangs over the religious legends of antiquity. The subject*, as it now stands, affords an ample field for indulging in pleasing theories and fanciful speculations; and as the probability increases of being able to trace all forms of divine worship to one sacred and primeval source, the inquiry in proportion becomes more interesting, and awakens a train of serious ideas in a reflecting mind.

It would be as unsatisfactory as tedious to attempt leading my reader through the mazes of mythological fable, and extravagant allegory, in which the Hindu religion, both Braminical and Buddhaic is envelop-

* General Vallancey, so justly celebrated for his knowledge of the antiquities of his country, has expressed his perfect conviction that the Hindus have been in Britain and in Ireland. See Major Ouseley's Oriental Collections, Vol. II. Much attention is certainly due to such respectable authority.

ed and obscured; it may be sufficient to observe, that the Birmans believe in the Metempsychosis, and that after having undergone a certain number of transmigrations, their souls will at last either be received into their Olympus on the mountain Meru*, or be sent to suffer torments in a place of divine punishments. Mercy they hold to be the first attribute of the divinity; " Reverence be to thee, O God, in the form of Mercy!" and they worship God by extending mercy unto all his creatures.

The laws of the Birmans, like their religion, are Hindu; in fact, there is no separating their laws from their religion: di-

---

* Meru properly denotes the pole, and, according to the learned Captain Wilford, it is the celestial north pole of the Hundus, round which they place the garden of Indra, and describe it as the seat of delight.

vine authority revealed to Menu the sacred principles in a hundred thousand
slocas, or verses; Menu promulgated the
code; numerous commentaries* on Menu
were composed by the Munis, or old phi-
losophers, whose treatises constitute the
Dherma Sastra, or body of law.

The Birmans generaly call their code
Derma Sath, or Sastra; it is one among
the many commentaries on Menu: I was
so fortunate as to procure a translation of
the most remarkable passages, which were
rendered into Latin by Padre Vincentius
Sangermano, and, to my great surprise, I

---

* The code of Geutoo laws, translated by Mr. Halhed,
I am informed, is a compilation from the different commentaries on Menu, who was " the grandson of Bramah,
the first of created beings," and whose work, as translated by Sir William Jones, is the ground of all Hindu
jurisprudence.

found it to correspond closely with a Persian version of the Arracan code, which is now in my possession. From the inquiries to which this circumstance gave rise, I learned, that the laws, as well as the religion of the Birmans, had found their way into the Ava country from Arracan, and came originally from Ceylon : The Birman system of jurisprudence is replete with sound morality, and, in my opinion, is distinguished above any other Hindu

---

* As an incontestible proof that the Birmans acknowledge the superior antiquity of the Cingalese, and the reception of their religion and laws from that quarter, the King of Ava has sent, within these few years, at separate times two messengers, persons of learning and respectability, to Ceylon, to procure the original books on which their tenets are founded ; and, in one instance, the Birman minister made an official application to the Governor General of India, to protect and assist the person charged with the commission.

commentary for perspicuity and good
sense; it provides specifically for almost
every species of crime that can be committed, and adds a copious chapter of prece-
dents and decisions to guide the inexperi-
enced in cases where there is doubt and
difficulty. Trial by ordeal and inpreca-
tion are the only absurd passages in the
Book; but on the subject of women it is,
to an European, offensively indecent: like
the immortal Menu, it tells the magistrate
their duty, in language austere, manly,
and energetic; and the exhortation at the
close is at once noble and pious: the following extracts will serve as a specimen:

   " A country may be said to resemble
" milk, in which oppression is like to wa-
" ter; when water is mingled with milk,
" its sweetness immediately vanishes, in
" the same manner oppression destroys a

" fair and flourishing country. The royal
" Surkaab* will only inhabit the clearest
" stream ; so a prince can never prosper
" in a distracted empire. By drinking pure
" milk the body is strengthened and the
" palate is gratified ; but when mingled
" with water, pleasure no longer is found,
" and the springs of health gradually de-
" cline.

" A wise prince resembles a sharp sword,
" which at a single stroke cuts through a
" pillar with such keenness that the fabric
" still remains unshaken ; with equal keen-
" ness his discernment will penetrate ad-
" vice.

" A wise prince is dear to his people, as
" the physician is to the sick man ; as light
" to those that are in darkness ; as unex-

---

* Bittern. Surkaab is a Persian term, used by the Mo-
hommedan translator.

" pected sight to the eyes of the blind; as
" is the full moon on a wintry night, and
" milk to the infant from the breast of its
" mother."

The commentator then proceeds to de-
nounce tremendous judgments against an
oppressive prince and a corrupt judge; the
latter is thus curiously menaced :

" The punishment of his crimes, who
" judges iniquitously, and decides falsely,
" shall be greater than though he had
" slain one thousand women, one hundred
" priests, or one thousand horses."

The book concludes as follows :

" Thus have the learned spoken, and
" thus have the wise decreed, that litiga-
" tion may cease among men, and conten-
" tion be banished the land : and let all
" magistrates and judges expound the laws
" as they are herein written; and, to the

" extent of their understanding, and ac-
" cording to the dictates of their consci-
" ence, pronounce judgment agreeably to
" the tenor of this book : let the welfare of
" their country, and the benefit of their fel-
" low-creatures, be their continual study,
" and the sole object of their attention : let
" them ever be mindful of the supreme
" dignity of the Roulah* and the Bramans,
" and pay them that reverence which is
" due to their sacred characters : let them
" observe becoming respect towards all
" men, and they shall shield the weak
" from oppression, support the helpless,
" and, in particular cases, mitigate the
" severity of avenging justice.

" It shall be the duty of a prince, and
" the magistrates of a prince, wisely to
" regulate the internal police of the empire,

---

* The Arracan for Rhakaan.

" to assist and befriend the peasants, mer-
" chants, farmers, and those who follow
" trades, that they may daily increase in
" worldly wealth and happiness: they shall
" promote all works of charity, encourage
" the opulent to relieve the poor, and libe-
" rally contribute to pious and laudable
" purposes: and whatsoever good works
" shall be promoted by their influence and
" example, whatsoever shall be given in
" charity, and whatsoever benefit shall
" accrue to mankind from their endea-
" vours, it shall all be preserved in the re-
" cords of heaven, one-sixth part of which,
" though the deeds be the deeds of others,
" yet shall it be ascribed unto them ; and
" at the last day, at the solemn and awful
" hour of judgment, the recording spirit
" shall produce them, inscribed on the a-
" damantine tablet of human actions. But,

" on the other hand, if the prosperity of
" the nation be neglected, if justice be suf-
" fered to lie dormant, if tumults arise and
" robberies are committed, if rapine and
" foul assassination stalk along the plains,
" all crimes that shall be thus perpetrated
" through their remissness, one-sixth part
" shall be brought to their account, and
" fall with weighty vengeance on their
" heads; the dreadful consequences of
" which surpass the power of tongue to
" utter, or of pen to express."

Laws, thus dictated by religion, are, I
believe, in general, conscientiously admi-
nistered. The criminal jurisprudence of
the Birmans is lenient in particular cases,
but rigorous in others; whoever is found
guilty of undue assumption of power, or
of any crime that indicates a treason-
able intent, is punished by the severest

tortures. The first commission of theft does not incur the penalty of death, unless the amount stolen be above 800 kiat, or tackal, about 100l. or attended with circumstances of atrocity, such as murder or mutilation. In the former case, the culprit has a round mark imprinted on each cheek by gunpowder and punctuation, and on his breast the word thief, with the article stolen; for the second offence he is deprived of an arm; but the third inevitably produces capital punishment: decapitation is the mode by which criminals suffer, in the performance of which the Birman executioners are exceedingly skilful.

The city of Ummerapoora is divided into four distinct subordinate jurisdictions, in each of which a Maywoon presides. This officer, who, in the provinces, is a viceroy, in the metropolis resembles a mayor, and holds a civil and criminal court of justice; in capital cases he transmits the evidence in writing, with his opinion, to the Lotoo, or grand chamber of consultation, where the council of state assembles; the council, after close examination into the documents, reports upon them to the King, who either pardons the offender, or orders execution of the sentence: the Maywoon is obliged to attend in person, and see the punishment carried into effect.

Civil suits may be transferred from the courts of the Maywoons to the Lotoo; this removal, however, is attended with a heavy expence. There are regular established lawyers, who conduct causes, and plead: eight only are licensed to plead in the Lotoo; they are called Ameendozaan: the usual fee is five tackal, equal to sixteen shillings; but the government has large profits on all suits that are brought into court.

There is no country of the East in which the royal establishment is arranged with more minute attention than in the Birman court; it is splendid without being wasteful, and numerous without confusion; the most distinguished members, when I was at the capital, were: the Sovereign, his principal Queen, entitled Nandoh Praw, by whom he has not any sons; his second wife Myack Nandoh, by whom he has two sons; the Engy Teekien*, or Prince Royal, and Pee Teekien, or Prince of Prome. The princes of Tongho, Bassien, and Pagahm, are by favourite concubines. Meedah Praw is a princess of high dignity, and mother of the chief queen. The prince

---

* Often called Engy Praw.

royal is married, and has a son and two daughters all young; the son takes precedence of his uncles, the crown descending to the male heirs in a direct line. These were the principal personages of the Birman royal family.

Next in rank to the princes of the blood royal, are the Woongees*, or chief ministers of state. The established number is four, but the place of one has long been vacant: these form the great ruling council of the nation; they sit in the Lotoo, or imperial hall of consultation, every day, except on the Birman sabbath, from twelve till three or four o'clock, or later, as there happens to be business; they issue mandates to the Maywoons, or viceroys of the different provinces; they con-

---

* Woon signifies burthen; the compound word implies, Bearer of th Great Burthen.

trol every department of the state, and, in fact, govern the empire, subject always to the pleasure of the King, whose will is absolute, and power undefined.

To assist in the administration of affairs, four officers, called Woondocks are associated with the Woongees, but of far inferior authority; they sit in the Lotoo in a deliberative capacity, having no vote; they give their opinions, and may record their dissent from any measure that is proposed; but the Woongees decide: the Woondocks, however, are frequently employed to carry into execution business of great public importance.

Four Attawoops, or ministers of the interior, possess a great degree of influence, that sometimes counteracts with success the views and wishes of the Woongees; these the King selects to be his privy

D

counsellors, from their talents, and the opinion he entertains of their integrity: they have access to him at all times; a privilege which the principal Woongee does not enjoy.

There are four chief secretaries, called Sere-dogees, who have numerous writers or inferior Serees under them.

Four Nachaangee sit in the Lotoo, take notes, and report whatever is transacted.

Four Sandobgaan regulate all ceremonials, introduce strangers of rank into the royal presence, and are the bearers of messages from the council of state to the King.

There are nine Sandozians, or readers, whose business it is to read all official writings, petitions, &c.—Every document, in which the public is concerned, or that is brought before the council in the Lotoo is read aloud.

The four Maywoons, already mentioned, are restricted to the magisterial superintendance of their respective quarters of the city; they have nothing farther to do with the Lotoo, than to obey the commands they receive from thence.

The Assaywoon, or paymaster-general, is also an officer of high importance; the place is at present held by one of the Woongees, who is called Assay Woongee.

There are several other officers of distinction, who bear no ostensible share in the administration of public affairs, such as the Daywoon, or King's armour-bearer; the Chaingeewoon, or master of the elephants; also the Woons of the Queen's household, and that of the Prince royal. Each of the junior princes has a distinct establishment.

In the Birman government there are no hereditary dignities or employments; all honours and offices, on the demise of the possessor, revert to the crown.

The tseloe, or chain, is the badge of the order of nobility, of which there are different degrees, distinguished by the number of strings or small chains that compose the ornament; these strings are fastened by bosses where they unite: three of open chains-work is the lowest rank; three of neatly twisted wire is the next; then of six, of nine, and of twelve: no subject is ever honoured with a higher degree than twelve; the King alone wears twenty-four.

It has already been noticed, that almost every article of use, as well as ornament, particularly in their dress, indicates the rank of the owner; the shape of the beetle-box, which is carried by an attendant after a Birman of distinction wherever he goes, his ear-rings, cap of ceremony, horse furniture, even the metal of which his spitting-pot and drinking-cup are made (which is of gold, denote him to be a man of high consideration,) all are indicative of the gradations of society; and woe be unto him that assumes the insignia of a degree which is not his legitimate right!

The court dress of the Birman nobility is very becoming; it consists of a long robe, either of flowered satin or velvet, reaching to the ankles, with an open collar and loose sleeves; over this there is a scarf, or flowing mantle, that hangs from the shoulders; and on their heads they wear high caps made of velvet, either plain, or of silk embroidered with flowers of gold, according to the rank of the wearer. Ear-rings are a part of male dress; persons of condition use tubes of gold about three inches long, and as thick as a large quill, which expands at one end like the mouth of a speaking-trumpet; others wear a heavy mass of gold beaten into a plate, and rolled up; this lump of metal forms a large orifice in the lobe of the ear, and drags it down by the weight to the extent sometimes of two inches. The women likewise have their distinguished paraphernalia; their hair is tied in a bunch at the top of the head, and bound round with a fillet, the embroidery and ornaments of which express their respective ranks; a short shift reaches to the pit of the stomach, is drawn tight by strings, and supports the breasts; over that is a loose jacket with close sleeves; round their waist they roll a long piece of silk, or cloth, which, reaching to their feet, and some-

times trailing on the ground, encircles
them twice, and is then tucked in. When
women of condition go abroad, they put on
a silk sash, resembling a long shawl, which
crosses their bosom, and is thrown over
the shoulders, gracefully flowing on each
side. The lowest class of females often
wear only a single garment, in the form of
a sheet, which, wrapped round the body,
and tucked in under the arm, crosses their
breasts; which it scarcely conceals, and
descends to their ankles: thus, when they
walk, the bottom of the cloth, where it
overlaps is necessarily opened by the pro-
trusion of the leg, and displays to a side view
as high as the middle of the thigh; such
an exposure in the opinion of an European,
bears an indecent appearance, although it
excites no such idea in the people themselves.—There is an idle and disgusting

story related by some writers, respecting
the origin of this fashion, which, being
wholly unfounded, does not deserve repetition: it has been the established national
mode of dress from time immemorial; an i
every woman, when walking, must shew
great part of her leg, as what may be called their petticoat, is always open in front,
instead of being closed by a seam.

Women, in full dress, stain the palms
of their hands and their nails of a red
colour, for which they use a vegetable
juice, and strew on their bosoms powder
of sandal-wood, or of a bark called Sun-
neka, with which some rub their faces.
Both men and women tinge the edges of
their eye-lids and their teeth with black;
this latter operation gives to their mouths a
very unseemly appearance in the eyes of
an European, which is not diminished by

their being constantly filled with beetle-leaf. Men of rank wear, in common dress, a tight coat, with long sleeves made of muslin or of extremely fine nankeen, which is manufactured in the country; also a silk wrapper, that encircles the waist; the working class are usually naked to the middle, but in the cold season a mantle or vest of European broad cloth is highly prized.

The Birmans, in their features, bear a nearer resemblance to the Chinese than to the natives of Hindustan. The women, especially in the northern part of the empire, are fairer than Hindu females, but not so delicately formed; they are, however, well made, and in general inclined to corpulence: their hair is black, coarse, and long. The men are not tall in stature, but active and athletic; they have a very

E

youthful appearance, from the custom of
plucking their breads instead of using the
razor. they tattoo their thighs and arms.
into various fantastic shapes and figures,
which they believe operate as a charm
against the weapons of their enemies.
Neither the men nor the women are so
cleanly in their persons as the Hindus of
India, among whom diurnal ablution is a
religious as well as a moral duty. Girls
are taught, at an early age, to turn their
arms in such a manner as to make them
appear distorted: when the arm is extend-
ed the elbow is inverted, the inside of
the joint being protruded, and the external
part bending inwards; from this cause,
the pendant arm in the plates seems as if it
were broken; the representation is, never-
theless, perfectly faithful

Marriages among the Birmans are not
contracted until the parties attain the age

of puberty : the contract is purely civil ; the ecclesiastical jurisdiction having nothing to do with it. The law prohibits polygamy, and recognizes but one wife, who is denominated Mica ; concubinage, however, is admitted to an unlimited extent. A man may repudiate his wife under particular circumstances, but the process is attended with a heavy expence. Concubines, living in the same house with the legitimate wife, are, by law, obliged to perform menial services for her ; and when she goes abroad, they attend her, bearing her waterflaggon, beetle-box, fan, &c. When a husband dies, his concubines, if bound in servitude to him, become the property of the surviving widow, unless he shall have emancipated them by a specific act previous to his decease. When a young man is desirous to espouse a girl, his mother, or nearest female relation, first makes the proposal in private; if the suit be well received, a party of his friends proceed to the house of the parents of the maiden, with whom they adjust the dotal portion. On the morning of the bridal-day the bridegroom sends to the lady three loongees, or lower garments, three tubbecks, or sashes, and three pieces of white muslin; such jewels also, ear-rings and bracelets, as his circumstances will admit: a feast is prepared by the parents of the bride, and formal writings are executed; the new-married couple eat out of the same dish, the bridegroom presents the bride with some lapack, or pickled tea, which she accepts, and returns the compliment: thus ends the ceremony without any of that subsequent riot* and resistance

---

* See Marsden's Account of Sumatra, page 230.

on the part of the young lady and her female friends, with which the Sumatrian
damsels oppose the privileges of an ardent
bridegroom.

When a man dies intestate, three-fourths
of his property go to his children, born in
wedlock, but not in equal proportions;
and one-fourth to the widow, who is the
guardian both of the property and the
children, until the latter attain the age of
maturity. A Birman funeral is solemniz-
ed with much religious parade, and external demonstration of grief: the corpse is
carried on a bier, on men's shoulders; the
procession moves slowly; the relations attend in mourning; and women, hired for
the occasion, precede the body, and chant
a dirge-like air. The Birmans burn their
dead, unless the deceased is a pauper, in
which case he is either buried or cast into

the river, as the ceremony of burning is
very expensive. The bier is placed on a
funeral pile six or eight feet high, made of
billets of dried wood laid across, with in-
tervals to admit a circulation of air and increase the flame. The Rhahaans walk
round the pile, reciting prayers to Gaudma, until the fire reaches the body, when
the whole is quickly reduced to ashes: the
bones are afterwards gathered and deposited in a grave. Persons of high distinction, such as the Seredaw, or chief eccle-
siastic of a province, a Maywoon, a Woongee, or a member of the royal family, are
embalmed, and their remains preserved six
weeks or two months after decease before
they are committed to the funeral pile:
during this period the body is laid in state
in some kioum or religious building; but
at the capital it is placed in a sacred ba-

loon, beautifully ornamented with gilding, and exclusively appropriated to that pious purpose. I was told, that honey is the principal ingredient made use of to preserve the body from putrefaction.

Of the population of the Birman dominions I could only form a conclusion from the information I received of the number of cities, towns, and villages in the empire; these, I was assured by a person who might be supposed to know, and had no motive for deceiving me, amount to eight thousand, not including the recent addition of Arracan. If this be true, which I have no reason to doubt, and we suppose each town, on an average, to contain three hundred houses, and each house six persons, the result will determine the population at fourteen millions four hundred thousand. Few of the inhabitants live in solitary habitations; they mostly form themselves into small societies, and their dwellings thus collected compose their Ruas, or villages: if, therefore, we reekon their numbers, including Arracan, at seventeen millions, the calculation may not be widely erroneous; I believe it rather falls short of, than exceeds the truth. After all, however, it is mere conjecture, as I have no better data for my guidance than what I have related.

"With regard to the revenue of the Birman state, I confess myself to be without the means of forming even a rough estimate of the amount. According to the sacred law in the chapter which treats of the Duties of a Monarch, Dhasaméda, or a tenth of all produce, is the proportion which is to be exacted as the authorized due of the government; and one-tenth is the amount

of the King's duty on all foreign goods imported into his dominions. The revenue
arising from the customs on imports, and
from internal produce, is mostly taken in
kind; a small part of which is converted
into cash, the rest is distributed, as received, in lieu of salaries, to the various de-
pendants of the court. Princes of the
blood, high officers of state, and provincial
governors, receive grants of provinces, cities, villages, and farms, to support their
dignity, and as a remuneration of their services: the rents of these assignments they
collect for their own benefit. Money, except on pressing emergency, is never dis-
bursed from the royal coffers; to one man
the fees of an office are allotted; to another a station where certain imposts are
collected; a third has land; each in proportion to the importance of his respective

F

employment : by these donations, they are
not only bound in their own personal servitude, but likewise in that of all their de-
pendants ; they are called slaves of the
King, and in turn their vassals are denominated slaves to them : the condition of
these grants include also services of war
as well as the duties of office. Thus the
Birman government exhibits almost a faithful picture of Europe in the darker ages,
when, on the decline of the Roman empire,
the principles of feodal dependance were
established by barbarians from the north.

Although it seems difficult, and perhaps
impossible, under such a system, to ascer-
tain, in any standard currency, the amount
of the royal revenue, yet the riches which
the Birman monarch is said to possess are
immense ; a supposition that may readily
be admitted, when it is considered that a

very small share of what enters his exche-quer returns into circulation. The hoard-ing of money is a favourite maxim of oriental state policy; an eastern potentate cannot be brought to comprehend that the diffusion of property among his subjects is a surer source of wealth to himself, and of security to his throne, than the posses-sion of Lydian treasures, locked up in vaults, and concealed in secret recesses, contrived by sordid avarice and foolish cunning.

A *further Account of the Birman Domi-*
nions and adjacent Countries, from
Dalrymple's Oriental Repertory.

In the beginning of the 17th century, it
appears both English and Dutch had considerable commerce in the Birman dominions; the English had establishments at
Syrian, at Prome, at Ava, and on the bor-
ders of China, probably at Prammoo. The
Dutch by an inscription, in Teutonick
characters, lately found at Negrais, on the
tomb of a Dutch Colonel, who died in
1607, appear then to have possession of
that Island, of which the Natives are said
to have an obscure tradition.

The exact year of our admission into, or
expulsion from this country, does not appear from any memoirs I have seen;
though there is, in them, some reason to

conjecture, the last happened before the middle of the 17th century.

It may be here proper to observe that this country contains two Nations, the Birmans and Peguers.

The Peguers resemble the Malays, in their appearance and disposition, though more industrious; they cut their hair round before and the back-part, from their ears to the crown of their head, is shaved in a semicircle.

The men are lusty, and particularly paint their thighs, as has been observed, not in figures of beasts, &c. as would seem, but like the Meangis.

The Birmans have more similitude to the Arabians in the features ; but are darker in complexion than the Peguers. The Birmans are much more numerous than the Peguers, and more addicted to com-

merce; even in Pegu their numbers are
100 to 1 : they punctuate themselves, and,
rubbing gunpowder into the wound, give
such marks as remain ever after ; they are
of a tawny complexion, though the women
who are not much exposed, if not white,
are at least fair : the common women un-
dergo all drudgery, and are very homely.

There is another people in this country
called Carianners, whiter than either, distinguished into Birman and Pegu Carianners ; they live in the woods, in small societies, of 10 or 12 houses ; are not want-
ing in industry, though it goes no farther
than to procure them an annual subsist-
ence.

They are remarkable for their perfect
morality, but have no apparent religion ;
when asked if they believe the existence of
any superior being, they replied, that the

Birman and Pegu Tallopins told them so, but that they knew nothing about it.

It is customary with them to place a duck, or Fowl, with some rice, upon the grave of every deceased person; when asked on this also, they give no reply, but that it is customary. When any person dies they abandon the house, and build another.

The first dominion the Birmans had over Pegu, was about 300 years ago, when called in against Siam; but the Peguers never had any Authority over the Ava dominions 'till above a century after, when having thrown off the Birman yoke, and reduced the then independant states of Dalla, Martaban, &c. They marched to Ava and were very near taking that capital, however in that they failed; and being then again subdued, it is

the common report, in that country, that
only 7 Peguers, of each sex, were saved
from general Massacre that ensued ; It
cannot be imagined that after so general a
destruction, they could for a long time
make head against the Birmans, and indeed I can find no traces of any Revolt
'till 1740, in which year being supported
from Siam, a body of many thousand Peguers and their Allies entered Syrian on
the 4th December, and massacred the
Birmans of every age, sex and condition ; the same was done in the provinces
of Tavoy, Martaban, Tongoo and Prone
(or Prome) where the Birman Government was established, so that the conquest
of Ava, the only place left, was thought
certain ; Simento the Pegue chief, who
was King, having heard of this success,
sent a letter to the English Resident, ad-

vising him of the motives which had induced them to rise at all hazards, viz. The grievous oppressions the Peguers laboured under, and the massacre of them and the Siamese, intended by the Birman Government.

In 1741, a narrative of the progress of the war, from the commencement of hostilities to that time, was transmitted to Fort St. George; but from having no opportunity to recur to that narrative, I can say nothing of the war, 'till 1743. On the 10th November the Birmans regained Syrian, the Peguers having deserted it, but on the 13th the Pegu army returned and put the Birmans to flight; as the factory was now withdrawn, I cannot give you any account of what followed, farther than that hostilities continued, generally with ill success on the part of the Birmans, 'till April

G

1752, when Ava was taken: this is the commencement of the æra of the Pegu dominion over Ava, as the King was made prisoner, and the empire overturned; however the Pegu affairs gradually declined from this time, 'till October 1754, when they put the captive King to death; thenceforward they hurried to destruction, as that event joined all the Birmans under the banner of the antagonist, whose superior courage and conduct, completed the conquest by taking Pegu in 1757.

In 1787, Captain Weldon with whom Dampier mentions to have made a voyage to Tonqueen, went in the Curtana to Mergui, to declare war against Siam. In his return he touched at Negrais, of which he made a survey; and having destroyed some Siamese inscriptions and huts, took possession of the Islands, and hoisted Colour ; and left an inscription, on tin, of his proceedings. In this voyage he surveyed the Nicobars also, which survey, with the history of them by a Spanish Priest, who had resided there many years, was sent to the Company, and may possibly be still extant.

I can't help taking notice of another prophecy, universally received, (which greatly impeded any grant from the Pegu Government, though the Birman Prince seems to despise it.) It is a report, that, about this period, a nation wearing hats, shall conquer the Empire, and overthrow the Government.—I mention this, that I might have an opportunity of observing, that in all countries, there are vulgar prophecies which will ensure success to the politician, who is observant of them: You cannot but remember how long disaffected persons called the Battle of Preston, in 1745, by the name of Gladsmuir, from the old prediction of Thomas, the Rhimer, who says of the decisive Battle :

On Gosford Green it shall be seen
By Gladsmuir Tree, the Battle be.

Give me leave to express my opinion, that to the person who could make an elephant white, if he added to it the distinction of a remarkable hat, the conquest of the Birman empire whould be certain.

To drop politics and treat of geography !

The Birman Empire to the south is bordered by the Siamese dominions : on the East it has Yunnan, a province of China, part of Laos and of Siam; to the North is Thibet, between which is a mountainous tract, according to the Chinese, inhabited by a savage people, whom they name Lisse.

On the West is the Sea, and the tributary States of Arracan and Cassay ; though it is uncertain whether since the Revolution, Arracan has yet submitted.

The Kingdom of Birmans, I conceive, includes Ava, Prome, Persaim, Pegu, and many other smaller districts, Tavoy, Martaban, Reys, which lies between the two last; and Tammoo towards Siam; perhaps Arracan ought also to be included, as it is reported to have been subject to them. The countries mentioned in the title, were only tributary, though several of them have advantaged by the disjointed Government of late, and thrown off their Allegiance; Allum Praw declared he would oblige them all to submit, before he sheathed the sword; but it is reported he abandoned himself to women, after he completed the Conquest of Pegu, and probably will not be so much inclined to commence a new war, as he seemed to be of prosecuting the old one.

As I cannot have recourse to many writers, who mention these countries, it would be impossible to be very minute in my description, nor indeed would such task be agreeable to the plan I have laid down ; their general situation and produce, is all I have in view, except when I am able to give some information not to be met in Books.

The Birman dominions yield Gold, Silver, Iron, Tin, Copper, Lead, Allum, Elephant's Teeth, some Pepper and Cardamums, Musk, Lacs, Furs, Precious Stones, Elephants, Grain, Hartal, Turmerick, Cutch, Wax, Earth-Oil and Wood-Oil, plenty of Cotton and Silk, and Salt-petre.

The last, produced in the countries between Prome and Ava, may be had in any quantities ; if permission be granted to export it, (which seems implied by the treaty

concluded in 1757.) It behoves us atten-
tively to endeavour preventing other Nations from being concerned in this branch of
commerce, as the exclusive privilege granted in Bengal will be inestimably beneficial, if the like can be obtained in Pegu ; besides will lower the price at Bengal, and
secure a sufficiency in case of any accident
in that Province ; it ought however to be
observed, that a sample sent to Madras
some years ago, was found much inferior
to what is produced in Bengal.

The common price of Rice formerly was
20 baskets, three of which make a bag, for
a Rupee; now it is about 15 only.

The country for 20 miles round Persaim,
is represented as capable of producing
Rice sufficient to supply the Coast of Coromandel, from Pondicherry to Masulapa-
tam, 20 miles inland.

Vast quantities of Raw Silk may be obtained from this and the adjacent countries. The prohibition of exporting it from China, demands our attention to enquire whence it may be had. And as all these countries produce plenty of Cotton, I presume an encouragement to the cultivation of it, will be the means of securing in a few years a sufficient quantity for the Investment in Bengal, and on the Coromandel Coast ; not to mention the great probability that a very considerable Investment of Piece Goods may be had in this country ; the people are described as very industrious, and so addicted to weaving, that scarce a house from Prince to Peasant, is without a Loom.

Formerly considerable quantities of Woollen Goods were carried thither from the Coromandel Coast, and as they must there have been purchased at an advanced price, it is evident that they would have turned to better account, had they been imported immediately from Europe.

The Jesuits, who have published an Account of Cochin-China, report that the inhabitants of Laos, carry on a considerable traffick with Thibet; this must be done either through the province of Yunnan, or through the dominions of the Birmans; either way it is evident a trade may be carried on by the English, with these respective countries; Laos in Mr. Bowyear's opinion will take off considerable quantities of Woollen Goods: and, if we may judge from the situation and climate of Thibet, there is no room to doubt that a good vent will be found for them there. Yunnan also, and the adjoining provinces, will probably take off large quantities; although being so distant from Canton, and the Sea

H

Coasts of China, they can at present have
very little share in the Europe trade; especially as the numberless Hopo-houses,
by the exactions, as well as by the established duties, will not admit Goods to be
transported so far, but at an enormous expence: This branch seems formerly to
have been driven, from the establishment at
Prainmoo. Nor are we to suppose Wool-
lens the only article that may be introduced,
many others from Europe, as well as from
various parts of India, undoubtedly will
find a vent.

Tavoy produces Tin in large quantities,
Rice in plenty, and some Cardamums;
there is in this country a gold Mine, which
is reported to be valuable; it abounds, as
well as all others on this side of India,
with Timber: the natives are of an indo-
lent disposition. The King of this country

offered the English an establishment in
1752. The terms I shall insert, as they
may yield you some satisfaction, though
the offer was rather neglected than refused.
He required of the Company 102 pieces
of Cannon, 3 covids and one span long,
four of 5 covids and one span, 100 mus-
quets, 1000 carties of powder, and a like
quantity of shot, and that 50 men should
be kept there for his defence, at the company's charge, so long as the settlement
was continued: And that the succours,
necessary at any time, for the preservation
of his Country, should also be transported
at their expence; besides which he was to
have an annual present, so long as they
continued the establishment; though the
value of that present was not specified.
On these considerations the following privileges were offered: 1st. The company

to have the refusal of all the Tin in his country, and private Merchants only to have what the Company did not chuse to purchase. 2d. They were allowed to purchase as much Grain as their ships may require. 3d. Leave to build Vessels, and to cut the timber necessary for this purpose, as well as for lading ships. And on these conditions it was stipulated, that all their ships should be free from paying Customs, or making presents.

That these terms ought not to have been accepted, is beyond dispute; but it is not so clear that a settlement in this country, on more advantageous terms, would not be beneficial; certainly, however, at this time it was improper to insert in a proposed Treaty with Pegu, that the Company would assist them against Tovoy; not only as these had proffered their friendship, which was not rejected, but as the Pegu Government might very sensibly have urged, that it was not against Tavoy, but against the Birmans, they desired assistance, but in truth, that Treaty is a miserable piece, wrote in the stile of a country Attorney's Clerk, and unworthy the notice of a politician.

I remember to have seen some years ago a particular chart of the Tavoy River; it is very deep within, but whether there be water enough at the entrance for a large ship I cannot possibly say.

1st July 1759. The next adjacent country to be mentioned is Siam; it hardly merits notice, if their behaviour did not deserve chastisement, which may turn to more advantage than the trade whilst subject to such impositions, as at present, under so injurious a Government.

The productions of this country are prodigious quantities of Grain, Cotton, Benjamin, Sandal, Aguala, and Sapan Wood, Antimony, Tin, Lead, Iron, Loadstones, Gold and Silver, Suppheridas, Emeralds, Agates, Chrystal, Marble, and Tambank.

An English Vessel was very lately seized, and the crew murdered in a Siamese Port; the Captain fortunately had narrowly escaped; in consequence of his report, remonstrance was made to the King; and a resolution taken of making reprisals if satisfaction was not given; so notorious an act of treachery ought not be forgiven, merely from receiving pecuniary satisfaction; as Siam has no force, and would be a very valuable acquisition to any European nation, either in whole, or in part, though the trade will yield but

little advantage under the present circumstances.

The several descriptions of this country,
in print, will convey a better idea of it
than any thing I can say in general; but
as I have been informed of some circumstances regarding Mergui, by a gentleman
who was lately there, I must beg leave to
repeat these circumstances.

There is still the remains here of an
old English Fort, but the Siamese have no
force, except a few old guns, which they
would abandon at the first appearance of
an enemy. The River was formerly navi-
gable to Tenasserim, where the Portu-
guese had a Fort, but the communication
is only open for boats at present; whether
the navigation of the River was spoiled by
accident, or intentionally, is uncertain: it
is reported there is a communication with

Junk ceylon, from Tenasserim for boats, by the Rivers within land.

Provisions are extremely plenty and cheap; a dozen, or 20 fowls may be bought for a Tical (little more than $\frac{1}{2}$ a crown) fish are very fine, and equally cheap; and Rice may be bought for about 12 Pagodas a garce; the price of Rice on the Coromandel Coast is generally above 30 and sometimes even 80 Pagodas per garce: the commodities in chief demand, are Salt, Iron, Tabacco, and Michlepatam Chintz. For Salt, which generally is from 3 to 3¼ Pagodas per garce, on the Coast of Coromandel, they give in return at Mergui 3 of Rice for 1 of Salt. A bundle of Tabacco which will cost about a Pagoda on the Coast of Coromandel, will some-times sell for the value of 10 or 12 at Mergui; the Chintz, and other fine painted

goods will, if the Market is not overstock-
ed, find immediate vent, and sell for 100
per Cent. It is evident from hence, that
were the country under better Government,
it would yield no contemptible trade; especially in that sure article of Grain; but
there is another consideration of weight in
regard to Mergui. The French have frequently of late years gone thither, and
should they be kept out of Bengal and Pegu, it can scarcely be doubted they will
fix themselves here, as it is so situated as
to admit an early arrival on the Coromandel Coast, abounding in Grain which they
may transport with the greatest conveni-
ency to Pondicherry, and as there is the
greatest plenty of fine Timber, and many
Carpenters, which must greatly expedite
and falicitate the repairs, which may be
required by their fleets in war.

I

In this place I beg leave to observe that the gentleman above mentioned assured me that they pass from Mergui to Judia, in about 3 weeks during the floods, when the Rivers overflowing great extent of country, they pass the greatest part of the way by water on rafts. In the dry season, they are almost double this time.

" Extracted from Captain Cox's Journal
of a Residence in the Birman Empire,
and more particularly at the Court of
Amarapoorah".

———◆———

July 17, 1797. In the morning I sent my
interpreter to the woondock's, to learn if he
had made any advance in my business,
and to inform him that I only waited for
the expiration of the five days to pursue
my own resolutions, in case his endeavours
failed. He informed Mr. Keys that he had
not as yet been able to effect any thing,
but meant to make an effort again this day;
and requested that I would have patience
for a day or two longer. He again requested that I would not think of requiring
leave to retire, as it might be attended with
very bad consequences; and strongly ad-
vised, that I should accept the king's

commission as Resident at Rangoon; saying, that it would infallibly lead to his
granting all my requests. He was more
moderate and flattering in his discourse
than he had ever been before. He, however, renewed the subject of the Birman
claims on Dacca, &c., but lowered the demand to one-tenth of the revenues. He
said it was evident that we were dubious
of our right, by Captain Symes having so
strenuously urged the building of a ches-
koy on the Naaf, to mark that river as the
boundary between the two countries. Had
the Naaf been the proper boundary, there
was no occasion for Captain Symes's agi-
tating the subject; we had betrayed our
consciousness of our want of right by his
solicitude on that occasion. These argu-
ments shew how necessary caution is in
treating with this people: every act of

complaisance is construed into fear, and every concession is but a stimulus to their arrogance and insolence. They have publicly said, that 3,000 men would be sufficient to wrest from us the province they claim; and the mhee whoonghee has even pledged himself to effect the service with that number. I forgot to mention, because it scarcely attracted my notice at the time, that, at my last interview with the mhee whoonghee, when he was enforcing the necessity of adding the article relative to his Birman majesty agreeing to be friends with the English, &c., he said that, his majesty had not as yet consented to admit us among the number of his friends; and that, unless he did consent, it was probable, that he and I, who are now such good friends, might soon be opposed to each other as enemies, in the armies of our respective countries. It would be endless to state all the impertinencies that have been indirectly conveyed to me; every art has been essayed to intimidate me; but the little effect attending these efforts has afforded the aggressors but little encouragement. The contagion has spread to our usual visitants, who have deserted us these several days past. In the course of yesterday I drew up a final address for the members of the footo, and, with great difficulty, got it translated into the Birman language. As I have never positively refused to receive his majesty's commission, but endeavoured only to evade it, as nugatory and embarrassing, yet, as complaisance therein may tend to reconciliation, I mean to inform them in the morning, that I have no objection to receive it as preliminary measure.

July 18. In conformity with my resolution of yesterday, I sent my interpreter
early in the morning to the woondock, to
inform him, that I had no objection to receiving his majesty's commission. He was
evidently well pleased with this notice;
waived the idea of my going to the looto
for it, and told my interpreter, that if he
and the mewjerry would go to the looto
at noon, it should be delivered to them;
added, that I might depend on its being
followed by a grant of all I wished. He
also informed him, that a gilt boat had
been despatched express, yesterday at
noon, for the mayhoon of Hunzawuddy,
who was ordered to repair to court without his family, with all expedition, in an
express-boat, and that he would be here
in twenty-five days. As I have ever been
willing to meet these people half way,

whenever I have found them disposed to treat me with civility, I determined to send my private assistant, Mr. Burnett, with an escort of sepoys, and two sontaburdars, with a silver salver and gold cloth, to receive and bring his majesty's commission to me. I accordingly sent notice of my intention and was informed that the court were well pleased with this intended respectful mark of my attention.

At half-past eleven A. M. I sent Mr. Burnett &c., to the looto; the escort, &c., was stopped at the outer gate of the palace, and Mr. Burnett was conducted to the looto, and seated in the line of sandoghans, and other inferior officers of the court. They kept him waiting till three o'clock, when he was informed that the commission could not be delivered to him; that I myself must come to the looto to receive it, and to take an oath of allegiance to his majesty. Previous to this, the three woondocks present, offered to take the commission to my house, but to this the mhee whoonghee objected, and insisted on the necessity of my attending in person at the looto. He sent for my interpreter to say something to him, and he went round to his excellency to hear what he had to say, when his excellency said he wished him to take a message to me; but as I had given Mr Burnett strict orders to enter into no discussion, but confine himself solely to the receiving the commission; he told him that his orders confined him to receiving the commission, and that if it was not to be delivered to him, he begged leave to retire. The whoonghee then desired, that he would wait a little and take their messenger with him. Mr. Burnett again inform-

K

ed him, that his orders were positive, and that he must retire. He accordingly returned home immediately. No messenger came to me, as expected, from the looto; but about eight o'clock at night, the mhee whoonghee's confidential writer came to my house, and informed me that his excellency wished to see me at his house for a quarter of an hour the next morning. I returned for answer, that I was sorry I could not do myself the pleasure of waiting on his excellency, as I had already been at his house six or seven times since his return, without effect, as he would never listen to me, and hardly treated me with common attention.

July 19. In the morning I sent my interpreter to inform the woondock, that as the five days were now elapsed I intended sending Mr. Burnett to receive the looto's final answer to my message of the tenth instant. He said it was unnecessary sending Mr. Burnett, as the court had already determined not to lay my memorials before his majesty; and that as to permission for my retiring to Rangoon, it would not be granted. My interpreter then told him, that having met with so indelicate a disappointment yesterday about the commission, I had determined not to send again for it, but would receive it with every respect if sent to my house by proper officers. The woondock acknowledged that I was justified in this conduct, and laid all the blame on the mhee whoonghee. He then asked if the whoonghee had not sent for me yesterday evening? Mr. Burnett replied in the affirmative, and informed him of my reply. He rejoined, that he was not surprised at my resentment, as he had heard

from others of his improper conduct towards me; but added, the Resident
should not take offence at him, as every
one knows him to be a rude low man, destitute of politeness.

At half-past eleven A. M. I sent Mr.
Burnett with the interpreter to the looto,
but when they arrived at the gate of the
palace they were refused admittance. After some difficulty, the porter permitted
the interpreter to go to the looto, to give
notice that Mr. Burnett was waiting at the
gate ; orders were then given for his admittance. When he came to the looto, he
found only the first woondock there ; he
was directed to take his former place, and
desired to sit down. The woondock then
asked him what his business was at the
looto? He replied, he had a message to
deliver. The woondock told him, that he

had better go to the nakhan's house, and deliver the message to him. Mr. Burnett replied, that his business was with the loo-to, and not with the nakhan; that he came to receive an answer to the message he had delivered some days before, and to deliver another from me. The woondock told him, as the court was not yet assembled, and he had not obtained regular permission to come to the court, he had better retire and wait till it was formed. While Mr. Burnett was seated in the loo-to, the mhee whoonghee's writer, who had brought me the message the evening before, came up to him, and in an insolent tone of voice asked, why I had not waited on the whoonghee agreeably to the intimation he had given me? adding that the whoonghee had expected me all the morning. Mr. Burnett very properly would

not permit any answer to be given to his
insolent interrogation, and retired. As to
wait in the gate-way would have been rather irksome and improper, he went to the
house of a merchant near at hand, and
waited there till he saw the pacaam whoonghee (who according to the Birman ete-
quette, being first in rank goes last) go to
the looto ; he then again presented himself
at the gate, and was stopped as before.
An officer of the court passing by obtained permission for the interpreter to go on
to inform the court of Mr. B.'s being in
waiting. When he came to the looto, the
mhee whoonghee in an imperious tone of
voice called out to the nakhan, that he
would not permit my interpreter to deliver any message there ; that if the strangers had any message to deliver, it must
be through Moncourtuse, the king's trans-

lator: he added, I sent for that man,
meaning me, to come to me this morning
and he did not attend. He made no offer,
however, to send for Moncourtuse, and as
he would not permit the interpreter to
speak, he retired and informed Mr. Burnett of the mhee whoonghee's orders: he
in consequence returned home.

About noon a Mr. Reeves, an English
merchant, arrived here from Rangoon with
private adventure, to try the market. He
requested permission to wait on me to-
morrow.

July 20. In the morning Mr. Reeves,
merchant, waited on me. He informed
me, that he had had a good deal of trou-
ble from the chokeys, notwithstanding the
mayhoon of Hunzawuddy had given him
some of his people as a guard, and a pass-
port.

In the evening, a favourite relation of the king's grandson, called to see Mr. Keys, &c., and expressed a wish to see me; however, in the present state of my business, I did not think it proper to gratify him.

July 21. His majesty, immediately after his return to Amarapoorah, issued orders for the currency of the pice I brought from Bengal, and prohibited the currency of silver and lead in the Bazars; but established no rate at which the pice were to pass, nor had he coined any, or even issued the whole of those I brought (one lack,) nor provided any medium in the room of the silver currency. Under these circumstances the people were much distressed, and obliged to substitute rice instead of lead for small purchases in the provision markets. Privately, silver still continued current, notwithstanding the prohibition, and the officers of government winked at it to prevent the stagnation of all business. This forbearance coming to the knowledge of his majesty, he this day suspended the whoonghees from the exercise of their offices, exposed them to the sun in the palace-yard from ten till four o'clock, with pieces of silver round their necks, and was with difficulty prevailed on by their humble submission to refrain from severer punishment. He has not however pardoned them, and has ordered that the looto shall continue shut. The two mayhoons or governors of the fort are confined in the firehouse loaded with irons; and the former orders respecting the currency directed to be enforced with the greatest rigour. I understand he is coining rupees and pice in the palace.

July 22. In the morning I sent my interpreter to the first woondock to ask his
advice, how I should convey to his majesty my wishes to return to Rangoon; he
told him it was impossible to convey a
letter to his majesty on the subject, and
that I must patiently wait the arrival of
the mayhoon of Hunzawuddy, who had
been sent for express, and was expected
at court in twenty days. He confirmed
the accounts of his majesty's displeasure
and punishment of the whoonghees. From
him Mr. R. also learnt, that the new regu-
lations respecting the coinage were as
follows:—For 100 ticals weight of silver,
two and a half per cent. standard delivered into the royal mint, 60 pieces each
weighing one tical, would be given in exchange; that 20 of the pice I brought from
Bengal were to be given in exchange for

one of those coined ticals, or 40 pieces of his majesty's coinage. Now supposing the ticals issued from the mint to be of the same standard as the silver paid in, or $2\frac{1}{2}$ per cent. worse than pure silver, he will gain at the rate of $66\frac{1}{3}$ per cent. on the silver; and as the copper piece I brought cost him only one tical, 5 per cent. silver, for 81, or 83 for one tical of $2\frac{1}{2}$ per cent. silver, and he sells them at the rate of one tical for 20, his gain on those pice will be 315 per cent., or in plainer language, the pice he bought for 100 ticals, he will sell for 415 ticals. His gain on the pice of his own coinage will amount to about one-third more; but if we take into consideration the advanced or nominal value of his new silver coinage. the profits on the issue of the Bengal pice will be enormous indeed. On the lack of pice, he will gain

7,318 ticals, five per cent. silver, or 8781 sicca rupees, at the rate of 593 per cent. This statement will serve as a proof of the extreme avarice, despotism and ignorance, which holds dominion here.

Ten men, principal merchants, have been condemned to lose their heads for paying, and receiving, silver bullion as heretofore contrary to his majesty's orders.

July 24. In the morning I sent my interpreter to the engai's whoon, to learn his sentiments respecting my situation, &c.: he confirmed the account of the mayhoon's having been sent for, but was in other respects rather reserved, as my interpreter told him his calling was accidental. One of my washermen having absconded, I availed myself of the occasion to send the interpreter to the pacaam whoonghee's; he received him with kindness, and promised his endeavours towards finding my man. He also mentioned that the may-hoon, would soon be here, and inquired after my health, &c. The men who were to have been executed, have obtained a reprieve at the intercession of the courtiers; and the mayhoons of Amarapoorah have also been liberated.

July 25. In the morning I sent my interpreter to the engai's whoon, to request his advice, as to the best means of conveying a letter to his majesty, to obtain his permission for my retiring to Rangoon. This message brought on a conversation respecting late occurrences. He expressed his sorrow for the disappointments and treatment that I had experienced, and promised to consult with the Enga Tekaing on the subject and let me know the result. From the engai's whoon, my interpreter went to the pacaam whoonghee's to remind him of his promise to send men to apprehend my washerman. He received him with great affability, and entered on the discussion of my business, in their loose way: in general, a mere repetition of all the idle nousense which I have so often detailed; but concluded with saying, there were now only two difficulties to surmount; one was the establishing a chokee on the Naaf, the other, my taking the oath of allegiance to his majesty. In respect to the first, it is the first time I ever heard of it from them as a point of contest; and as to the latter, as it has never been proposed to me regularly, I have never delivered my sentiments on it. While my interpreter was with him, one of the engai's confidential servants came in, and began the old story of the encroaching spirit of the

English. The king's merchant, my visitant, took up the cudgels in our defence, and exposed the infamy and ignorance of our calumniators (the Mahomedans, &c.) with success, the pacaam whoonghee joining him. He said, he knew the English were a brave and faithful people, but that the French were not to be trusted. He had experienced their conduct at Syrian, and bared his arm to shew were he had been wounded by a musket-ball, when their ships attacked the Birman camp. The engai's man confessed, he had received his intelligence from the Malabars and Mahomedans.

July 26. In the morning I sent my interpreter to the engai's whoon for his answer to my message of yesterday. He excused himself on account of the heavy rain which had prevented his seeing the prince.

He desired he would give his compliments
to me, and say, that he would consider
himself much obliged to me, if I would
forgive Mr. Moncourtuse, pledging himself,
for his good behaviour in future. As I had
no further view in' the displeasure I had
shewn against Moncourtuse, than to keep
him in awe of me, and to prevent his mis-
chievous tricks, and as I was happy to
have an opportunity of fixing an obligation
on the engai's whoon, I therefore determined to acquiesce in his request. About
eleven A. M. he sent for my interpreter, and
I ordered him to tell the engai's whoon,
that I was happy in having an opportunity
of obliging him ; and notwithstanding the
just cause I had to be angry with Moncourtuse, at his instance I would forget all
that was past, on promise of better behaviour for the future. He appeared pleased

with this concession, and sent Mr. Moncourtuse to me with my interpreter whom
he desired to tell me, that he would punish
Mr. Moncourtuse himself in the event of
his behaving ill again. Mr. Moncourtuse
presented himself with a half-penitent, half-
brazen face, in which impudence and consci-
ous guilt were struggling for the ascendency.
I waived listening to his defence, and con-
tented myself with cautioning him to be
more guarded in future, as he regarded
his own interests and safety. I then detailed to him the heads of the several of-
fensive measures, and follies of the Birman
ministers, pointing out the disgrace which
attached to them as a nation, for practis-
ing them on me, and their pernicious ten-
dency. I was very full on these subjects,
knowing that he would communicate them
again. I pretended that I had given up

M

all idea of transacting business with them, and only wanted permission to retire to Rangoon; which I desired he would request the engai's whoon to obtain for me.

As I have the strongest conviction, that this man has throughout acted in concert with the members of government, I may reasonably attribute his present submission to some projected change of operations; but all conjecture is in vain where folly plans, and caprice sways.

July 27. In the evening Mr. Moncourtuse called on me, and informed me that the engai's whoon had not yet had an opportunity of speaking to the engai tekaing, but expected to have some conversation with him at night.

I learn that the pacaam whoonghee had represented to his majesty the distress of his people for want of a current medium of commerce; that the shops were shut up, and the bazars unsupplied, and entreated that he would permit flowered silver to pass current, until such time as a sufficient quantity of rupees and pice were coined and issued from the royal mint. His majesty waived the discourse, yet it was hoped he would yield to this reasonable request.

July 28. The hopes entertained yesterday of his majesty's permitting flowered silver to be current has vanished. On the pacaam whoonghee renewing the request this day, he was extremely indignant, and forbade him to speak again on the subject. Mr. Reeves, the English merchant, has not been able in consequence to dispose of any of his goods, although the merchants are willing to buy, but have not the means of paying him. In the evening Moncour-

tuse waited on me, and informed me from
the engai's whoon, that he had represented my case to the prince, who in reply
said, he would not interfere; that I must
first apply to the looto, and that when
they had laid my request before his majesty and his opinion was asked, he would
then exert his interest in my favour; so that
my hopes from him are no more: as I am
fully resolved never to give the looto a-
nother opportunity of insulting me, or to
hold any interview with them, until they
have amply apologized for their conduct
towards me, and therefore I directed Mr.
Moncourtuse to inform the prince, that
if any benefit could arise from my
yielding, I should not hesitate a mo-
ment; but I have had too frequent oppor-
tunities of observing, that politeness and
moderation, on my part only tends to pro-

voke insolence on theirs: and were I to
succumb in the least under my present circumstances, I am fully convinced they
would trample on me immediately. The
drift of Moncourtuse's apparent submission is now sufficiently evident; they wish to
employ him as the instrument of humbling
me; but I trust they will in this, as well as
all their other sagacious projects, find themselves disappointed.

Description of the Kingdom of Assam, taken from the ALEMGEERNAMEH *of* MOHAM- MED CAZIM, *and translated by* HENRY VANSITTART, *Esq.*

Extracted from Mr. Gladwin's Asiatick Miscellany; the notes signed T. are taken from a more recent trans- lation of the same tract, published in the 11th number of the Calcutta Telegraph.

ASSAM[*], which lies to the north-east of Bengal, is divided into two parts of the river Birhmapoter, that flows from Khita.

[*] Mons. De Lisle, in his History of India beyond the Ganges, calls this country Achem or Acham, and tells us, that it was formerly a part of the empire of Ava, un- der the king of Pegue, who had no less than twenty king- doms in his dominions, among which was Assam ; but he does not tell his readers how or when this country be- came tributary to the Pegue monarch, or by what means it at lenght shook off its allegiance. It should seem that Assam was first discovered by the Moguls in

The northern portion is called Otercol;
and the southern Dekincol *. Otercol be-
gins at Gowahutty, which is the boundary
of his majesty's territorial possesions†, and

Aureng Zeeb's time by sailing up the large river Laqui,
which (says a contemporary of De Lisle's, Mons. Mar-
tinia,) rises from the lake Chiamay, and after a course
from east to west, bends southwards, and falls with di-
vers mouths into the eastern branch of the Ganges. Our
present author, in his account of Assam, makes no
mention whatever, either of the river Laqui, or the Lake
Chiamay; both certainly, worthy of note, the one for
its navigation—the other, its astonishing size, which according to Luy's, is 180 leagues in compass. —T.

* Neither Tarvenia De Lisle, Moll, Fytch or Hamil-
ton, make mention of either of these divisions; nor are
their names to be found in Bowen's or Rennel's map—T.

† Our author, no doubt means on the northen side of
Assam; but he gives us no boundaries to the east, west,
or south, unless he means those mountains, and that chain
of hills which we find him speak of immediately after. De

terminates in mountains inhabited by a
tribe called Meeri Mechmi. Dekincol ex-
tends from the village Sidea to the hills of
Serinagurf. The most famous mountains
to the northward of Otercol are those of
Duleh and Landah ; and to the southward
of Dekincol are those of Manruss, situated
four days journey above Ghergong to which
the Rajah retreated. There is another chain
of hills which is inhabited by a tribe called
Nanec, who pay no revenue to the Rajah,
but profess allegiance to him, and obey a
few of his orders. But the Zemleh* tribe
entirely independent of him, and, whenever

Lisle's boundaries of Assam are certainly laid down in a
much more clear and satisfactory manner ; it has, says this
writer, Tartary and Boutan on the north Tipras, on the
south part of China on the east and of the Mogul on the
west from which it is divided by the river Arracan.

* In another copy this tribe is called Dufleh.

they find an opportunity, plunder the country contiguous to their mountains. Assam is of an oblong figure; its length is about 200 standard coss*; and its breadth, from the northern to the southern mountains, about eight days journey †. From Gowahutty to Ghergong is 75 standard coss; and from thence it is fifteen days journey to Khoten, which was the residence of Peeran Wiseh ‡. but is now called A-

---

* Four hundred English miles—a coss being equal to two miles.

† Mons. De Lisle makes it 90 German leagues from N. E. to S. W. and about 40 where broadest.——T.

‡ According to Khondemir, Peeran Wiseh was one of the Nobles of Afrasiab, King of Turan, contemporary with Kaicaus, second Prince of the Kianian Dynasty. In the Ferhung Jehangeery, and Berham Kates, (two Persian dictionaries,) Peeran is described as one of the Pehlovan, or heroes of Turan, and General under Afrasiab, the name of whose father was Wiseh.

va*, and is the capital of the Rajah of Pegue, who considers himself of the posterity of that famous General. The first five days' journey from the mountains of Namrup is performed through forests, and over hills, which are arduous and difficult to pass. You then travel eastward to Ava, through a level and smooth country. To the northward is the plain of Khita, that has been before mentioned as the place from whence the Birhmapoter issues, which is afterwards fed by several rivers that flow from the southern mountains of Assam. The principal of these is the Dhonec, which has before occurred in this history.

* Here we have another note by the same Gentleman, who corrects our author in the mistake he makes, in calling Khoten "Ava."—Khoten lies to the north of Hemalaya; and Peeran Wiseh could never have seen Ava.—T.

It joins that broad river at the village Luckeigereh.

Between these rivers is an island, well inhabited, and in an excellent state of tillage: it contains a spacious, clear and pleasant country, extending to the distance of about fifty coss: the cultivated tract is bounded by a thick forest, which harbours elephants, and where those animals may be caught, as well as in four or five other forests of Assam. If there be occasion for them, five or six hundred elephants may be procured in a year*. Across the Dhonec, which is the side of Ghargong, is a wide, agreeable and level country, which delights the heart of the beholder: the whole face of it is marked with population and tillage; and it presents,

---

* Four elephants is the marriage portion to all women in Assam.

on every side, charming prospects of
ploughed fields, harvests, gardens, and
groves, all the island before described lies
in Dekincol. From the village Salagereh,
to the city of Ghergong, is a space of about
fifty coss, filled with such an uninterrupt-
ed range of gardens, plentifully stock-
ed with fruit-trees, that it appears as one
garden: within them are the houses of the
peasants, and a beautiful assemblage of
coloured and fragrant herbs, and of garden
and wild flowers blowing together.

As the country is overflowed in the rainy
season, a high and broad causeway has
been raised, for the convenience of tra-
vellers, from Salagereh to Ghergong, which
is the only uncultivated ground to be seen:
each side of this road is planted with
shady bamboos, the tops of which meet,
and are entwined. Amongst the fruits

which this country produces, are mangoes,
plantains, jacks, oranges, citrons, limes,
pine-apples, and punialeh, a species of
amileh, which has such an excellent flavour
that every person who tastes it prefers it
to the plumb. There are also cocoa-nut
trees, pepper-vines, beetle trees, and the
sadij *, in great plenty. The sugar-cane
excells in softness and sweetness, and is
of three colours, red black, and white.
There is ginger free from fibres, and beetle
leaf. The strength of vegetation, and fer-
tility of the soil, are such that whatever
seed is sown, or slips planted, they always
thrive. The environs of Ghergong fur-
nish small apricots, yams, and pomegra-

---

* The sadij is a long aromatic leaf, which has a pungent taste, and is called, in the Hindustanee language,
teez-paut. In our botanical book it bears the name
of Malabathrum, or the Indian leaf.

nates; but these articles are wild, and,
not assisted by cultivation and engraft-
ment, they are very indifferent. The principal crop of this country consists of rice
and mash*; adess is very scarce, and
wheat and barley are never sown. The
silks are excellent, and resemble those of
China; but they manufacture very few
more than are required for use. They are
successful in embroidering with flowers,
and in weaving velvet, and tautband, which
is a species of silk of which they make
tents and kenauts†. Salt is a very precious and scarce commodity; it is found at
the bottom of some of the hills, but of a
bitter and pungent quality; a better sort
is in common use, which is extracted from
the plaintain tree. The mountains, inha-

---

* Mash is a species of grain and adess, a kind of pea.

† Kenauts are walls made to surround tents.

bited by the tribe called Manec, produce
plenty of excellent lignum aloes, which a
society of the natives import every year,
into Assam, and barter for salt and grain.

This evil disposed race of mountaineers
are many degrees removed from the line of
humanity, and are destitute of the charac-
teristical properties of a man. They go
naked, from head to foot, and eat dogs,
cats, mice, snakes, rates, ants, locusts,
and every thing of this sort which they
can find. The hills of Namrup, Sidea, and
Luckeigereh, supply a fine species of lignum aloes, which sinks in water. Several
of the mountains contain musk-deer.

The country of Otercol, which is on the
northern side of the Birhmapoter, is in
the highest state of cultivation, and produces plenty of pepper, and beetle-nuts.
It even surpasses Dekincol in population

and tillage ; but as the latter contains a
greater tract of wild forests and places
difficult of access, the rulers of Assam
have chosen to reside in it for the convenience of control, and have errected in it the
capital of the kingdom. Otercol, from the
bank of the river to the foot of the mountains, which is a cold climate, and contains snow, is various ; but is no where
less than fifteen coss, nor more than forty-
five coss. The inhabitants of those mountains are strong, have a robust and respectable appearance, and are of a middling
size ; their complexions, like those of the
natives of all cold climates, are red and
white ; and they have also trees and fruits
peculiar to frigid regions. Near the fort
of Jum Dereh, which is on the side of
Gowahutty, is a chain of mountains called
the country of Dereng, all the inhabitants

of which resemble each other in appearance, manners and speech, but are distinguished by the names of their tribes and places of residence. Several of these hills produce musk, kataus*, bhoat†, peree, and two species of horses. called goont and tagnans. Gold and silver are procured here, as in the whole country of Assam, by washing the sand of the rivers : this indeed is one of the sources of revenue. It is supposed that 12,000 inhabitants, and some say 20,000, are employed in this occupation ; and it is a regulation.

* Kataus is thus described in the Borhaun Katea : "This word, in the language of Rome, is a sea-cow ; "the tail of which is hung upon the necks of horses, and "on the summit of standards. Some say it is a cow "which lives on the mountains of Khita." It here means the mountain-cow, which supplies the tail that is made into chowries.

† Bhoat and peree are two kinds of Blanket.

that each of these persons shall pay a fixed revenue of a *tola* * of gold to the Rajah. The people of Assam are a base and unprincipled nation, and have no fixed religion: they follow no rule but that of their own inclinations, and make the approbation of their own vicious minds the test of the propriety of their actions. They do not adopt any mode of worship practised either by Heathens or Mahommedans; nor do they concur in any of the known sects which prevail amongst mankind. Unlike the Pagans of Hindustan, they do not reject victuals which have been dressed by Mussulmen; and they abstain from no flesh except human. They even eat animals that have died a natural death; but, in consequence of not being used to the taste of ghee, they have such

---

* The weight of a rupee.

an antipathy to this article, that if they discover the least smell of it in their victuals, they have no relish for them. It is not their custom to veil their women; for even the wives of the Rajah do not conceal their faces from any person. The females perform their work in the open air, with their countenances exposed, and heads uncovered. The men have often four or five wives each, and publicly buy, sell, and change them. They shave their heads, beards and whiskers, and reproach and admonish every person who neglects this ceremony. Their language has not the least affinity with that of Bengal.*

---

* This is certainly a mistake, for the Bengallic is generally spoken in Assam; and we are told young Brahmins often come to Nuddeeah for instruction, and that their dialect is perfectly understood by the Bengal teachers.——T.

Their strength and courage are apparent
in their looks; but their ferocious manners, and brutal tempers, are also betrayed
by their physiognomy. They are superior
to most nations in corporeal force and hardy exertions. They are enterprising, savage, fond of war, vindictive, treacherous,
and deceitful: the virtues of compassion,
kindness, friendship, sincerity, truth, honour, good faith, shame, and purity of
morals, have been left out of their composition; the seeds of tenderness and humanity have not been sown in the field of
their frames: as they are destitute of the
mental garb of manly qualities, they are
also deficient in the dress of their bodies;
they tie a cloth round their heads, and a-
nother upon their loins, and throw a sheet
round their shoulders; but it is not customary in that country to wear turbans,

robes, drawers, or shoes. There are no
buildings of brick or stone, or with walls
of earth, except the gates of the city of
Ghergong, and some of their idolatrous
temples. The rich and poor construct
their habitations of wood, bamboos, and
straw. The Rajah, and his courtiers,
travel in stately litters (singasun); but the
opulent and respectable persons amongst
his subjects are carried in lower vehicles,
called doolies. Assam produces neither
horses?, camels, nor asses; but these cattle are sometimes brought thither from
other countries. The brutal inhabitants
from a congenial impulse, are fond of seeing and keeping asses, and buy and sell
them at a high price. But they discover

---

* As the author has asserted that two species of horses,
called goont and tagnans, are produced in Dereng, we
must suppose that this is a different country from Assam;

the greatest surprise at seeing a camel; and are so afraid of a horse, that if one trooper should attack a hundred armed Assamians, they would all throw down their arms and flee; or should they not be able to escape, they would surrender themselves prisoners; yet, should one of that detestable race encounter ten men of another nation on foot, he would defeat them.

The ancient inhabitants of this country are divided into two tribes, the Assamians and the Cultanians. The latter excel the former in all occupations, except war, and the conduct of hardy enterprises, in which the former are superior. A body guard of six or seven thousand Assamians, fierce as demons, of unshaken courage, and well provided with warlike arms and accoutrements, always keep watch near the Rajah's sleeping and sitting apartments; these are his loyal and confidential troops and patrol. The material weapons of this country are the musket, sword, spear, and arrow and bow of bamboo. In their forts and boats they have also plenty of cannon, zerbzun*, and ramchungee, in the management of which they are very expert.

Whenever any of the Rajahs, magistrates, or principal men die, they dig a large cave for the deceased, in which they inter his women, attendants and servants, and some of the magnificent equipage and useful furniture which he possessed in his life-time, such as elephant, gold and silver, bandcush (large fans), carpets, cloths, victuals, lamps, with a great deal of oil, and a torch-bearer; for they consider these articles as stores for a future state. They afterwards

---

* Swivels.

construct a strong roof over the cave upon thick timbers. The people of the army entered some of the old caves, and took out of them the value of 90.000 rupees in gold and silver. But an extraordinary circumstance is said to have happened, to which the mind of man can scarcely give credit, and the possibility of which is contradicted by daily experience. It is this: All the Nobles came to the Imperial General, and declared with universal agreement, that a golden beetle-stand was found in one of the caves that was dug eighty years before, which contained beetle-leaf quite green and fresh; but the authenticity of this story rests upon report*.

---

* About 125 miles to the S. W. on the Laquia river, just before it detaches one of its streams into the bay of Bengal, stands the city of Azoo, noted for being the seat of the tombs of the Kings of Assam; and here, in a spacious and magnificent temple, the monarchs are buri-

Ghergong has four gates constructed of stone and earth ; from each of which the Rajah's palace is distant three coss. The city is encompassed with a fence of bamboos ; and, within it, high and broad causways have been raised, for the convenience

---

ed, with the idol they worshipped when living, each having his own deity. Immense treasures of gold and silver are deposited in the royal vaults ; for though they think that such as lived good lives in the world will have plenty of all necessaries in the other, yet they believe the wicked suffer hunger and other miseries,—for which reason, not having so high an opinion of the sanctity of their Monarchs, as they of Boutan have of theirs, they bury riches with their Kings to supply their necessities, as well as his chief wives and officers, elephants, camels, hounds, &c. &c. which they believe will all rise to serve him in the other world.—I have, however, been assured by an officer who served in Assam under Col. Welsh, that the necessity of burying the royal elephants, camels, and hounds, is now dispensed with.

P

of passengers during the rainy season. In the front of every man's house is a garden, or some cultivated ground. This is a fortified city, which incloses villages and tilled fields. The Rajah's palace stands upon the bank of the Degoo, which flows through the city. This river is lined on each side with houses; and there is a small market, which contains no shop-keepers, except sellers of beetle: the reason is, that it is not customary for the inhabitants to buy provisions for daily use, because they lay up a stock for themselves which lasts them a year. The Rajah's palace is surrounded by a causeway, planted on each side with a close hedge of bamboos, which serves instead of a wall: on the outside there is a ditch which is always full of water. The circumference of the inclosure is one coss and fourteen jereebs. Within

it have been built lofty halls and spacious apartments for the Rajah, most of
them of wood, and a few of straw, which
are called chuppers. Amongst these is a
dewan khana, or public saloon, 150 cubits
long, and 40 broad, which is supported by
66 wooden pillars, placed at an interval of
about four cubits from each other. The Rajah's seat is adorned with lattice-work and
carving. Within and without have been
placed plates of brass, so well polished that,
when the rays of the sun strike upon them,
they shine like mirrors. It is an ascertained
fact, that 3000 carpenters, and 12,000 labourers were constantly employed in this
work, during two years, before it was finish-
ed. When the Rajah sits in his chamber, or
travels, instead of drums and trumpets,
they beat the dhole * and dand : the latter

---

* The dhole is a kind of drum, which is beat at each end.

is a round and thick instrument made of copper, and is certainly the same as the drum* which it was customary in the time of ancient kings to beat in battles and marches.

The Rajahs of this country have always raised the crest of pride and vain-glory, and displayed an ostentatious appearance of grandeur, and a numerous train of attendants and servants. They have not bowed the head of submission and obedience, nor have they paid tribute or revenue, to the most powerful monarch: but they have curbed the ambition, and checked the conquests of the most victorious princes of Hindustan. The solution of the difficulties attending a war against them, has baffled the penetration of heroes who

---

* This is a kind of kettle-drum, and is made of a composition of several metals.

have been styled conquerors of the world. Wherever an invading army has entered their territories, the Assamians have covered themselves in strong posts, and have distressed the enemy by stratagems, surprises and alarms, and by cutting off their provisions. If these means have failed, they have declined a battle in the field; but have carried the peasants into the mountains, burnt the grain, and left the country empty. But when the rainy season was set in upon the enemy, they have watched their opportunity to make excursions and vent their rage; the famished invaders have either become their prisoners, or been put to death. In this manner, powerful and numerous armies have been sunk in that whrilpool of destruction, and not a soul has escaped.

Formerly Hossein Shah, a King of Bengal, undertook an expedition against Assam, and carried with him a formidable force of cavalry, infantry and boats. The beginning of this invasion was crowned with victory. He entered the country, and erected the standard of superiority and conquest. The Rajah, being unable to encounter him in the field, evacuated the plains, and retreated to the mountains. Hossein left his son, with a large army to keep possession of the country, and returned ot Bengal. The rainy season commenced, and the roads were shut up by the inundation. The Rajah descended from the mountains, surrounded the Bengal army, skirmished with them, and cut off their provisions, till they were reduced to such straits that they were all in a short time either killed or made prisoners.

In the same manner Mahommed Shah, the son of Toglue Shah, who was King of several of the provinces of Hindustan, sent a well-appointed army of 100,000 cavalry to conquer Assam: but they were all devoted to oblivion in this country of enchantment, and no intelligence or vestige of them remained. Another army was dispatched to revenge this disaster; but when they arrived in Bengal, they were panicstruck, and shrunk from the enterprise; because if any passes the frontier into that district, he has not leave to return. In the same manner, none of the inhabitants of that country are able to come out of it; which is the reason that no accurate information has hitherto been obtained relative to that nation. The natives of Hindustan consider them wizards and magicians, and pronounce the name of that country in all their incantations and countercharms: they say, that every person who sets his foot there, is under the influence of witchcraft, and cannot find the road to return.

Jeidej Sing, the Rajah of Assam, bears the title of *Surgee*, or *Celestial*. Surg, in the Hindustanee language, means heaven. That frantic and vain-glorious Prince is so excessively foolish and mistaken, as to believe that his vicious ancestors were Sovereigns of the heavenly host; and that one of them, being inclined to visit the earth, descended by a golden ladder. After he had been employed some time in regulating and governing his new kingdom, he became so attached to it, that he fixed his abode in it, and never returned.

In short, when we consider the peculiar circumstances of Assam; that the country is spacious, populous, and hard to be pebe refuted; ... ... a peril and dangers, that the paths and roads are beset with difficulties; that the obstacles of the conquest of it are more than can be described; that the inhabitants are a savage race, ferocious in their manners, and brutal in their behaviour; that they are of a gigantic appearance, enterprising, intrepid, treacherous, well armed, and more numerous than can be conceived; that they resist and attack the enemy from secure posts, and are always prepared for battle; that they possess forts as high as heaven, garrisoned by brave soldiers, and plentifully supplied with warlike stores, the reduction of each of which would require a long space of time; that the way was obstructed by thick and dangerous bushes, and broad and boisterous rivers—when we consider these circumstances, we all ad-

mire that this country, by the aid of God,
and the auspices of his Majesty, was con-
quered by the imperial army and became
a place for erecting the standard of the
faith. The haughty and insolent heads
of several of the detestable Assamians, who
stretch the neck of pride and who are de-
void of religion and remote from God,
were bruised by the hoofs of the horses of
the victorious warriors. The Mussulman
heroes experienced the comfort of fighting
for their religion; and the blessings of it
reverted to the sovereignty of his just and
pious Majesty.

The Rajah, whose soul had been ensla-
ved by pride, and who had been bred up
in the habit of presuming on the stability
of his own government, never dreamt of
this reverse of fortune: but, being now
overtaken by the punishment due to his

crimes, fled, as has been before mentioned, with some of his nobles, attendants and family, and a few of his effects, to the mountains of Namrup. This spot, by its bad air and water, and confined space, is rendered the worst place in the world, or rather it is one of the pits of hell. The Rajah's officers and soldiers, by his orders, crossed the Dhonee, and settled in the spacious island between that and the Birhmapoter, which contains numerous forests and thickets. A few took refuge in other mountains, and watched an opportunity of committing hostilities.

Namrup is a country on the side of Dekincol, situated between three high mountains, at the distance of four days journey from Ghergong. It is remarkable for bad water, noxious air, and confined prospects. Whenever the Rajah used to be angry

c 2

with any of his subjects, he sent them thither. The roads are difficult to pass, in-
somuch that a foot traveller proceeds with
the greatest inconvenience. There is one
road wide enough for a horse; but the
beginning of it contains thick forests for
about half a coss. Afterwards there is a
defile, which is stony and full of water.
On each side is a mountain towering to
the sky.

" The Imperial General remained some
days in Ghergong, where he was employed
in regulating the affairs of the country, en-
couraging the peasants, and collecting the
effects of the Rajah. He repeatedly read
the knosbah, or prayer, containing the name
and titles of the prince of the age, king
of kings, Alumgeer, conqueror of the
world; and adorned the faces of the coins
with the same impression. At this time

there were heavy showers, accompanied
with violent wind, for two or three days;
and all the signs appeared of the rainy
season, which in that country sets in before
it does in Hindustan. The General exert-
ed himself in establishing posts, and fixing
guards, for keeping open the roads, and
supplying the army with provisions. He
thought now of securing himself during the
rains, and determined, after the sky should
be cleared from the clouds, and the lightning cease to illuminate the air, and the
swelling of the water should subside, that
the army should again be set in motion
against the Rajah and his attendants, and
be employed in delivering the country
from the evils of their existence.

The author then mentions several skir-
mishes which happened between the Rajah's
forces and the Imperial troops, in which the

latter were always victorious. He concludes thus:

At length all the villages of Dekincol fell into the possession of the imperial army. Several of the inhabitants and peasants, from the diffusion of the fame of his Majesty's kindness, tenderness, and justice, submitted to his government, and were protected in their habitations and property. The inhabitants of Otercol also became obedient to his commands. His Majesty rejoiced when he heard the news of this conquest, and rewarded the General with a costly dress, and other distinguishing marks of his favour.

The narrative to which this is a supplement, gives a concise history of the military expedition into Assam. In this description, the author has stopt at a

period when the imperial troops had possessed themselves of the capital, and were
masters of any part of the plain country
which they chose to occupy or over-run.
The sequel diminishes the credit of this
conquest, by shewing that it was temporary
and that the Rajah did not forget his usual
policy of harassing the invading army
during the rainy season. But this conduct
produced only the effect of distressing
and disgusting it with the service, instead
of absolutely destroying it, as his prede-
cessors had treated former adventurers.
Yet the conclusion of this war is far from
we.kening the panegyric whic   ho
has passed upon the Imperial General, to
whom a difference of situation afforded
an opportunity of displaying additional
virtues, and of closing that life with heroic

fortitude which he had always hazarded in the field with martial spirit. His name and titles were, Mere Jumleh, Moazzim Khan, Khan Khanan, Sepoy Salar.

An ACCOUNT *of the* PETROLEUM WELLS, *in the Burmah Dominions : extracted from the Journal of a Voyage from Rangoon up the River Erai-Wuddy to Amarapoorah, the present Capital of the Burmah Empire.*

— ◆ —

By Captain HIRAM Cox, Resident at Rangoon.

——

SATURDAY, January 7, 1797, wind easterly, sharp and cold, thick fog on the river until after sun-rise, when it evaporated as usual, but soon after collected again, and continued so dense till half-past eight *a. m.* that we could barely see the length of the boat.

Thermometer at sun-rise 52°, at noon 74°, in the evening 69°; general course of the river N. 20° W. main breadth from one to one and a half miles ; current about two and a half miles per hour.

East bank high, rugged, barren downs, with precipitous cliffs towards the river ; a free stone intermixed with strata of quartz, martial ore and red ochre; beech mode-rately shelving, covered with fragments of quartz, silex, petrifactions and red ochre, and with rocky points projecting from it into the river.

Western bank a range of low sandy is-lands, covered with a luxuriant growth of reeds. These at present narrow the stream to three quarters, and in some place to half a mile, but are overflowed in the rains; the main bank rather low and sandy, subject to be overflowed its whole breadth, about three miles to the foot of a range of low woody hills, which in point of vegetation, form an agreeable contrast to the eastern shore: these hills are bounded to the east-ward, at the distance of about twenty miles from the river, by an extensive range of high mountains clothed with wood to their summits.

At half past ten came to the lower town of Rangoon; a temple in it of the antique Hindu style of building.

At noon came to the centre town of Rangoon, (literally the town through which flows a river earth oil,) situated on the east bank of the river, in latitude 23° 26' N. and longitude 94° 45' 54" E. of Greenwich: Halted to examine the Wells of Petroleum.

The town has but a mean appearance, and several of its temples, of which there are great numbers, falling to ruins: the inhabitants, however, are well dressed, many of them with gold spiral ear ornaments; and are undoubtedly rich, from the great profit they derive from their oil wells, as will be seen below.

At two *p. m.* I set off from my boat, accompanied by the *mewthaghee*, or zemindar of the district, and several of the merchant proprietors, to view the wells. Our road led to the E. N. E. through dry beds of loose sand in the water courses, and over rugged arid downs and hillocks of the same soil as described above; the growth on them consisting of scattered plants of *Euphorbium*, the *Cassia* tree, which yields the *Terra Japonica*, commonly called *cutch* or *cut*, and used throughout India as a component part of a *beera* of *paun*, also a very durable timber for lining the oil wells, and lastly the hardy *Biar*, or wild plum, common in Hindustan.

The sky was cloudless, so that the sun shone on us with undiminished force, and being also unwell, I walked slowly, and as we were an hour in walking to the wells, I therefore conclude they are about three miles distant from the river; those we saw are scattered irregularly about the downs, at no great distance from each other, some perhaps not more than thirty or forty yards. At this particular place we were informed there are 180 wells, four or five miles to the N. E. 340 more.

In making a well, the hill is cut down so as to form a square table of fourteen or twenty feet for the crown of the well; and from this table a road is formed, by scarping away an inclined plain for the drawers to descend, in raising the excavated earth from the well, and subsequently the oil. The shaft is sunk of a square form, and lined, as the miner proceeds, with squares of cassia wood staves: these staves are about six feet long, six inches broad, and two thick; are rudely jointed and pinned

at right angles to each other, forming a
square frame about four and a half feet in
the clear for the uppermost ones, but more
contracted below. When the miner has
pierced six or more feet of the shaft, a
series of these square frames are piled on
each other, and regularly added to at
top ; the whole gradually sinking as he
deepens the shaft, and securing him against
the falling in of the sides.

The soil or strata to be pierced is nearly
such as I have described, the cliffs to be
on the margin of the river, that is, first, a
light sandy loam intermixed with fragments of quartz, silex &c.; second, a fri-
able sand stone, easily wrought, with thin
horizontal strata of a concrete of martial
ore, talc, and indurated argil,(the talc has
this singularity, it is denticulated, its lamini
being perpendicular to the horizontal lami-

ni of the argil, on which it is seated,) at from ten or fifteen feet from the surface, and from each other, as there are several of these veins in the great body of free stone. Thirdly at seventy cubits more or less from the surface, and immediately below the free stone, a pale blue argillaceous earth (schistus) impregnated with the petroleum, and smelling strongly of it. This they say is very difficult to work, and grows harder as they get deeper, ending in shist and slate, such as found covering veins of coal in Europe, &c. Below this shist, at the depth of about 130 cubits, is coal I procured some, intermixed with sulphur and pyrites, which had been taken from a well deepened a few days before my arrival, but deemed amongst them a rarity, the oil in general flowing at a smaller depth. They were piercing a new

well when I was there, had got to the
depth of eighty cubits, and expected oil at
ten or twenty cubits more.

The machinery used in drawing up the
rubbish, and afterwards the oil from the
well, is an axle crossing the centre of the
well, resting on two rude forked staun-
chions, with a revolving barrel on its centre,
like the nave of a wheel, in which is a
score for receiving the draw-rope; the bucket is of weaker work covered with dammer, and the labour of the drawers, in general three men, is facilitated by the descent of the inclined plain, as water is
drawn from deep wells in the interior of
Hindustan.

To receive the oil one man is stationed
at the brink of the well, who empties the
bucket into a channel made on the surface
of the earth, leading to a sunk jar, from

whence it is laded into smaller ones, and immediately carried down to the river either by coolies or on hackeries.

When a well grows dry, they deepen it. They say none are abandoned for barrenness. Even the death of a miner, from emphitic air, does not deter others from persisting in deepening them when dry. Two days before my arrival, a man was suffocated in one of the wells, yet they afterwards renewed their attempts without further accident. I recommended the trying the air with a candle, &c. but seemingly with little effect.

The oil is drawn pure from the wells, in the liquid state as used, without variation; but in the cold season it congeals in the open air, and always loses something of its fluidity; the temperature of the wells preserving it in a liquid state fit to be drawn.

A man who was lowered into a well 110 cubits in my presence, and immediately drawn up, perspired copiously at every pore: unforunately I had no other means of trying the temperature. The oil is of a dingy green, and odorous; it is used for lamps, and boiled with a little dammer (a resin of the country), for plying the timbers of houses, and the bottoms of boats, &c. which it preserves from decay and vermin; its medicinal properties known to the natives is as a lotion in cutaneous eruptions, and as an embrocation in bruises and rheumatic affectious.

The miners positively assured me that no water ever percolates through the earth into the wells, as had been sopposed. The rains in this part of the country are seldom heavy, and during the season a roof of thatch is thrown over the wells. The water that falls soon runs off to the river, and what penetrates into the earth is effectually prevented from descending to any great depth, by the increasing hardness of the oleaginous argil of shist; this will readily be admitted when it is known, that the coal mines at Whitby are worked below the harbour, and the roof of the galleries not more than fifty feet from the bed of the sea; the deficiency of rain in this tract may be owing to the high range of mountains to the eastward, which range parallel to the river, and arrest the clouds in their passage, as is the case on the eastern side of the peninsula of India.

Solicitous to obtain accurate information on a subject so interesting as this natural source of wealth, I had all the principal proprietors assembled on board my boat, and collected from them the following particulars ; the foregoing I learned at the wells, from the miners and others.

I endeavoured to guard against exaggeration, as well as to obviate the caution and reserve which mercantile men in all countries think it necessary to observe, when minutely questioned on subjects affecting their interests ; and I have reason to hope my information is not very distant from the truth.

The property of these wells is in the owners of the soil, natives of the country, and descends to the heir general as a kind of entailed hereditament, with which it is said government never interferes, and which no distress will induce them to alienate. One family perhaps will possess four or five wells. I heard of none who had more ; the generality of them have less, they are sunk by and wrought for the proprietors ;

the cost of sinking a new well is 2,000 tecals flowered silver of the country, or 2500 sicca rupees; and the annual average net profit 1000 tecals, or 1250 sicca rupees.

The contract price with the miners for sinking a well is as follows: for the 40 cubits they have 40 tecals, for the next 40 cubits 300 tecals, and beyond these 80 cubits to the oil they have from 30 to 50 tecals per. cubit, according to the depth (the Burmah cubit is nineteen inches English), taking the mean rate of 40 tecals per cubit, and 100 cubits as the general depth at which they come to oil, the remaining 20 cubits will cost 800 tecals, or the whole of the miners wages for sinking the shaft 1140 tecals; a well of 100 cubits will require 650 cassia staves, which, at 5 tecals per hundred, will cost 47½ tecals. Portage and workmanship in fitting them, may amount

to 100 tecals more; the levelling the hill
for the crown of the well, and making the
draw road, &c. according to the common
rate of labour in the country, will cost a-
bout 200 tecals, ropes, &c. and provisions
for the workmen, which are supplied by
the proprietor when making a new well,
expences of propitiatory sacrifices, and
perhaps a seigniorage fine to government
for permission to sink a new well, consume
the remaining $512\frac{1}{2}$ tecals: in deepening an
old well, they make the best bargain in
their power with the miners, who rate their
demand per cubit according to its depth or
danger from the heats or mephitic air.

The amount, produce, and wages of the
labourers who draw the oil, as stated to
me, I suspect was exaggerated ar erroneous from misinter pretation on both sides.

The average produce of each well, per
diem, they said, was 500 viss, or 1825 lbs.

avoirdupois, and that the labourers earned
upwards of eight tecals each per month ;
but I apprehend this was not meant as the
average produce, or wages for every day
or month throughout the year, as must appear from a further examination of the
subject ; where facts are dubious, we must
endeavour to obtain truth from internal
evidence. Each well is worked by four
men, and their wages is regulated by the
average produce of six days labour, of
which they have one sixth, or its value at
the rate of one and a quarter tecals per
hundred viss, the price of the oil at the
wells. The proprietor has an option of
paying their sixth in oil ; but I understand
he pays the value in money, and if so,
I think this is as fair a way of regulating
the wages of labour as any where practised ; for in proportion as the labourer

works he benefits, and gains only as he
benefits his employer. He can only do
injury by overworking himself, which is
not likely to happen to an Indian. No
provisions are allowed the oil drawers,
but the proprietors supply the ropes, &c.;
and lastly, the King's duty is a tenth of
the produce.

Now supposing a well to yield 500 viss
per diem throughout the year, deducting
one-sixth for the labourers and one-tenth for
the King, there will remain for the proprietor, rejecting fractions, 136,876 vis, which
at 1¼ tecals, the value at the wells, is equal
to 1710 tecals per annum. From this sum
there is to be deducted only a trifle for
draw ropes, &c. for I could not learn that
there was any further duties or expence to
be charged on the produce; but the merchants say they gain only a neat 100 tecals

per annum for each well, and as we advance we shall have reason to think they
have given the maximum rather than the
minimum of their profits; hence, therefore
we may infer, that the gross amount produce per annum is not 182,500 viss.

Further, the four labourer's share, or one
sixth, deducting the King's tithe, will be
2350 viss per month of thirty days, or in
money at the above price, 28 tecals 50
avas, or 7 tecals 12 avas each man per
month: but the wages of a common labourer in this part of the country, as the
same persons informed me, is only 5 tecals
per month when hired from day to day;
they also admitted that the labour of the oil
drawers was not harder than that of common labourers, and the employment no
way obnoxious to health. To me the smell
of the oil was fragrant and grateful, and

on being more indirectly questioned, (for on this part of the subject, perhaps owing to the minuteness of my inquiries, they were most reserved,) they allowed that their gain was not much greater than the common labourers of the country; nor is it reasonable to expect it should, for as there is no mystery in drawing of oil, no particular hardships endured, or risk of health, no compulsion or prevention pretended; and as it is the interest of the proprietors to get their work done at the cheapest rate, of course the numbers that would flock to so regular and profitable an employment would soon lower the rate of hire, nearly at least to the common wages of the country; besides I observed no appearance of affluence amongst the labourers; they were meanly lodged and clad, and fed coarsely, yet on rice, which in the upper province is an article of luxury, but on dry grains and indigenous roots of the nature of *Cassada*, collected in their wastes by their women and children. Further, it is not reasonable to suppose that these labourers worked constantly; nature always requires a respite, and will be obeyed, however much the desire of gain may stimulate; and this cause must more particularly operate in warm climates to produce what we often improperly call indolence. Even the rigid *Cato* emphatically says, that the man who has not time to be idle is a slave. A due consideration of this physical and moral necessity, ought perhaps to vindicate religious legislators from the reproaches too liberally bestowed on them for sanctioning relaxation: be that as it may, I think it is sufficiently apparent that the article of wages is also exaggerated, and that 500 viss must only be considered as the amount produce of working days, and not an average for every day in the year. The labour of the miners, as I have observed, above, is altogether distinct from the oil drawers, and their pay proportioned to their hardships and risks they endure.

Assuming therefore as data, the acknowledged profit of 1000 tecals per annum for each well, which we can hardly suppose exaggerated, as it would expose the proprietors to an additional tax, and the common wages of precarious employment in the country, that is one month with another, including holidays, the year round, 4½ tecals per month, as the pay of the oil drawers, which includes the two extremes of the question, it will make the average produce of each well per diem

360 viss, or 109,500 viss per annum, equal to 395,675lbs. avoirdupoise, or 173 tons 255lbs. or in liquid measure 793 hogsheads of 63 gallons each; and as there are 520 wells registered by government, the gross amount produce of the whole per annum will be 56,940,000 viss, or 92,781 tons 1590lbs. or 412,360 hogsheads ; worth at the wells, at one and a quarter tecals per hundred viss, 711,750 tecals, or 289,737 sicca rupees.

From the wells the oil is carried in small jars, by cooleys, or on carts, to the river; where it is delivered to the merchant exporter at 2 tecals per hundred viss, the value being enhanced three-eighths by the expence and risk of portage; therefore the gross value or profit to the country of the whole, deducting five per cent. for wastage, may be stated at 1,081,860 tecals, or

1,362,325 sicca rupees per annum, yielding
a direct revenue to the King of 136,232 sicca
rupees per annum, and perhaps thrice as
much more before it reaches the consumer,
besides the benefit the whole country must
derive from the productive industry called
into action, by the constant employment of so
large a capital on so gruff an article. There
were between 70 and 30 boats, average
burthen 60 tons each, loading oil at the
several wharfs, and others constantly coming and going while I was there. A number
of boats and men also find constant employment in providing the pots, &c. for the oil;
and the extent of this single branch of
internal commerce (for almost the whole is
consumed in the country) will serve to give
some insight into the internal commerce
and resources of the country.

At the wells the price of the oil is 7 annas 7 pice per 112lbs. avoirdupoise; at

the port of Rangoon it is sold at the rate of 3 sicca rupees 3 annas and 6 pice per 112lbs.; or per hogshead of 63 gallons, (weighing 504lbs.) 14 rupees 7 annas 9 pice, exclusive of the cask; or per Bengal bazar maund, 2 rupees 5 annas 8 pice; whereas the mustard seed and other vegetable oils sell at Rangoon at 11 rupees per bazar maund.

To conclude, this oil is a genuine petroleum, possessing all the properties of coal tar, being in fact the selfsame thing; the only difference is, that nature elaborates in the bowels of the earth, that for the Burmahs, for which European nations are obliged to the ingenuity of Lord DUNDONALD.

FINIS.

www.ingramcontent.com/pod-product-compliance
Lightning Source LLC
LaVergne TN
LVHW081353060426
835510LV00013B/1799